Singing the Bones Together

Singing the Bones Together

ANGELA
SHANNON

TIA CHUCHA PRESS
CHICAGO

Published by:
Tia Chucha Press
A Project of the Guild Complex
1212 N. Ashland Ave., Suite 211
Chicago IL 60622

Printed in the United States of America
10 9 8 7 6 5 4 3 2 1

ISBN 1-882688-28-7

Book Design: Jane Brunette
Cover Art: James Tanner

Distributed by:
Northwestern University Press
Chicago Distribution Center
11030 South Langley Avenue
Chicago IL 60628

*Tia Chucha Press is supported by the National Endowment for the Arts and
by general operating funds from the Guild Complex. The Guild Complex is
supported by the Alphawoods Foundation, CityArts Program 3 grant from the
City of Chicago Department of Cultural Affairs, Gaylord and Dorothy
Donnelly Foundation, The Harris Foundation, Illinois Arts Council, a state
agency, the Mayer & Morris Kaplan Family Foundation, John D. and
Catherine T. MacArthur Foundation, Northern Trust Company Prince
Charitable Trusts, and The Woods Fund of Chicago.*

Acknowledgments

Grateful acknowledgment is made to the editors of the following journals, in which some of the poems first appeared.

African Voices: "Flashback," "Sprouting Roots," "Coming Through,"
   "Shadow Man Chant"
Crab Orchard Review: "JoNelle," "Wet Oak"
Drumvoices Revue: "First Day"
Eyeball: "Young Girl Dancing"
Jackleg: "Coming Home"
Ploughshares: "Distant Rain"
TriQuarterly: "Sunday"
Water-Stone: "Sugar Blue"; "Hydrangeas"
Willow Review: "Doris"; "Hands" (which won the 1997 *Willow Review* Award)

"Freedom Baptist" also appears in *Power Lines: A Decade of Poetry from Chicago's Guild Complex,* edited by J. Parson-Nesbitt, M. Warr, and L. Rodriguez, published by Tia Chucha Press (1999).

"Hands," "Integration," "JoNelle," "Returning the Water," "Sunday," and "Wet Oak" also appear in *Beyond the Frontier: An Anthology of Contemporary African American Poetry for the 21st Century,* edited by E. Ethelbert Miller, published by Black Classic Press (2002).

"Sunday" also appears in *Step Into A World: The Global Anthology of the New Black Literature,* edited by Kevin Powell, published by Jossey Bass (2000), and *A Multicultural Reader, Collection One: Many Voices Literature Series,* edited by Rebecca Christian, published by Perfection Learning Corporation (2002).

"Carrying Home" and "Delivery" were commissioned by the Weisman Arts Museum in Minneapolis, Minnesota (March 2002).

Many of these poems were performed in the world premiere of *Root Woman,* at the Fleetwood-Jourdain Theatre under the direction of Phillip Edward VanLear in Evanston, Illinois (2001).

Thank yous:

I would like to thank the Illinois Arts Council for a 1998 Poetry Fellowship, and the Loft Literary Center for a 1998/99 Loft Mentor Award.

Thanks to the late Gwendolyn Brooks, for exemplifying poetry in how she lived, and Reginald Gibbons, who has been an inspiring mentor and friend.

My gratitude also to Joan Aleshire, M. Eliza Hamilton, Angela Jackson, Tyehimba Jess, Deborah Keenan, Mary Leader, Julie Parson-Nesbitt, Eugene Redmond, Luis Rodriguez, Ellen Bryant Voigt, Michael Warr.

I have abiding love and thanks to my family in-the-blood and in-the-large: Lisa and James Flagg, Gina and Oliver Spicer, Babette Shannon, Kenneth Shannon, Erma Coburn, Evadne Jones, Dr. Billie Wright Adams, Cynthia Williams, Cheri Cannon, Alana Tyler and a host of others.

Finally, thanks to my editor Olga Herrera, and designer Jane Brunette.

This book is possible because of the Guild Complex (Chicago) and the Loft (Minneapolis).

To God be the glory.

For
my parents,
Drs. John and Juel Shannon Smith,
my husband,
Rohan Preston,
and our daughters,
Adera and Adisa.

Contents

3

"So I prophesied as
was commanded:
and as I prophesied,
there was a noise,
and behold a shaking,
and the bones came together,
bone to his bone."

—Ezekiel 37:7

Remedies

for revival sing t he same song daily
start with sound simmering in throat

each day let voice grow louder
until the echo of Monday
meet Tuesday's hope

to remember mother never known
walk into a river backwards
eyes on sky   feet in water
keep afoot until water circles ears
ask river to re-call

lemongrass tea ginger root orange rinds
2 lumps of honey for withered soul

Sunday

It could have been the way the Southern man
in his navy suit and skin rocked
along the church wall, swaying to the tambourine
like an old man wobbling to blues.

Or the way Sister Nettie got the spirit
all in her feet and behind, quick-stepping
like an ant hill was under her toes,
shaking her head back and forth in disbelief—

Or the way Deacon Jones raised
both hands like the police were there,
and started pacing the pulpit—
a foreign street—looking for Jesus.

But something quick came over the church
when Walter's voice slid to his navel
and plucked a piece of umbilical cord,
tugging the notes from generations gone.

And a sister lost in the crowd screamed,
like when children have their first babies,
and screeching floated over the pews
and took the congregation rocking

back to the first cry we made
in this freedom-stealing country—
the first shout on the auction block,
and we tried to clap our way out of memory,

to stomp out the sound like sparks of fire
but it was already voiced (and the seer had said,
this child would be different).

Sugar Blue

With leather cap tipped over cat eyes,
a walking stick of a red man
wraps plum lips around his harmonica
and pushes breath inside it,

holding the horner like a baby bird:
something comes back to life,
begins flying around the jukejoint.

And in the corner talking to her third
shotglass, JoNelle smells Old Spice cologne,
feels piano fingers on her shoulders,
hears the laughter of her secret name.

Sugar snakes his spine into a whistle
and the Frisco train totters in,
with Paul Jones in new suit at the door,
and in his polished shoes you see

a summer storm stirring around
wife and children staying South,
this father arriving in Chicago.

Blue blows so strong his skin turns grey,
and somebody's lost child appears
playing jacks on the floor,
Doris moans, touches for her heart.

And a chain-gang's singing hangs
like spider webs in the air,
strong but only visible to the shadow
in the back humming along.

And by the time his blues is over
a circle is put back in place, folks
have their song tucked in their pockets
and a caged man tastes freedom again.

Flashback

Like an old woman retelling the same story,
the Mississippi River remembers and remembers.

A child enters the water—long toes, knobby knees,
five braids—full of play, no knowledge

of the river spelled by song, *M-i-crooked-letter-*
crooked-letter-i-hump-back-hump-back-i.

She shuts her eyes, throws her head back
for the water to hold. But the Mississippi's in a stupor.

Tell the river there are no captives here,
no coded spirituals, "stealing away to freedom,"

just a young girl no more than nine, unaware
the water suffers spells and flashbacks.

The child ducks under the water and hears
her grandmother gurgling in the current. She bobs up

for breath then dips deeper down.
Tell the river this is 2003, not 1785 nor 1849.

The Mississippi need not hide the girl under its waves.
There are no men at bay with shackles.

Tell the river to stop its ploy. Let the girl rise.
Somebody wake the river.

JoNelle

JoNelle don't believe in nakedness,
body isn't for all eyes, just
for body's own. She look in the mirror,

see Sadie standing on wood-slab,
left breast dripping, ghost men gawking,
circling like huffing vultures.

Evil barking demands: Squat. Lift.
Grin. Turn. Bend. Sadie's mind slipping
to sacred place as the paper women

and children glue their eyes
on her nostrils, ears, thighs. She has
no need to understand spit-words,

or why the duppy take fire-stick
and brand her heart, leaving a white
A. JoNelle imagines pulling up the ashoki

crumbled around Sadie's chained ankles,
crowning her hair with tie, and them walking
toward the land from whence they came.

Scattering Dreams

Dear Mama, I am sitting
under the umbrella tree
with paper and pencil stub.
Since I have learned to write,
angels crowd my shoulders
like Missy's wedding shawl.

Mama, when I am writing
flight enters my bones.
I'm planning the note
for our crossing over to Jordan.
I suspect we will look into the river,
see our faces, see our hands,

wavering on the water,
even see our broad feet
and claim ourselves,
this body belongs to me,
these are my ample arms,
my knobby knees, my knotted hair.

Mama, I come here on Sundays at sunrise
practicing the plan. First I write
my name, *Willa May*, then I write *Free*.
Then I seed my name.
I say *Willa May, Free* to leaves, to acorns,
to butterflies staring on the grass blades.

The soil under my heels starts whispering,
nudging me to stand, walk, get moving.
Seems like I can't stay on the ground,
those angels swooping around my pencil
are the same ones fluttering about my knees,
scattering dreams everywhere.

Emancipation

At dawn, the sun's a distant promise,
clouds squat among black mountains, for now,
exchanging lightning stories, thunder tales.

Like an uninvited guest, I rise to listen,
put on my faded T-shirt, old shorts
and running shoes and head to the field.

But the field is weighted with yesterday's rain,
my tracks sink into soil rooting out mud,
grass and dandelions. I become

brown on brown, soil on skin, the third time
circling the pasture. And suddenly,
I hear the huffing breath of someone behind

me and then the footsteps of many. They come
marching down from mountains through mist.
Some in chains, ropes dangling from their necks,

some missing arms. They come from behind
pine trees and cypress branches. They spring up
through the lavender and black-eyed susans.

Like wafers, words stick on their tongues.
A girl with cotton bows covering her dress
parts the crowd. She holds a folded piece of paper

in both palms as if it was the last canary.
Kneeling with ghosts huddled around me,
I wonder what keeps this world awake,

what so badly needs to be spoken.

First Signature

Marking them all over
the turquoise walls,
Adora practices her *X's.*
They are hundreds of blackbirds
taking flight. She draws a *vee*
on top and a *v* on the bottom,
a *v* on bottom and on top.

Where slanted lines come together,
she is the balancing spark
meeting in the middle,
dreaming a proper name.
In her scribbling, victory—
victory above us
and victory below.

When the Mountain Was a Young Hill

When the mountain was a young hill,
two tree trunks high and a creek wide,
we played hunt, running around the base,

traded rocks for fire branches.
When we looked toward different
galaxies, soil staining our knees and elbows,

tree bark coloring our faces,
you held out your hands and
I painted my eyes in your palm.

You drew yours in mine.
Then gathering berries and skins,
I walked toward the warmth,

through thick ferns draped in moss.
I never imagined the hill a mountain
or seeing you after centuries.

But there you were speaking at the museum,
chin pointing upward as if reading stars,
same grasshopper fingers clutching books,

the mountain pressed in your elbows,
the rocks I gave you next to your pen,
two black pupils in your waving palm.

Holding On

One moment I had two hands,
now, I am tending one.

I made it to the Book of Job
before they caught me reading

and cut the fingers on my right hand off—took
an ax, drew a thin line at my knuckles

and chopped like they were hacking chicken. Blood
shot up in their eyes, flowed like an angry river.

They left my thumb and I can hold.
A comb, pennies, paper, I can hold myself together.

Faithful Messenger

Light flickers like candles
when Maeola enters a room.
She's laid a healing hand on all asking,
but now, her mind flashes through the years.

Ghostly, she walks around trees,
trudges down to the river, the sky so heavy
she could pull it down like laundry,
one grey cloud at a time. Maeola thinks

over these twenty-seven years,
feels her fingers being whacked off,
sees her blood fountaining the sky.

At the bank, she holds up her stem,
folds to her knees, as she's done countless times.
Pleas and petitions start, turn
into murmurs and moans

then with an orange sunset,
the waves take them away,
like a faithful messenger.

Root Women

The humming women pour oil
in their palms—Emma, Ruth and Pearl.
Six hands cover all of her.
Wetness warms her forehead.
They circle in their *re-mem-ber*
stories, soothe with waves of prayer.

When Maeola comes to herself, she is
lying under oak branches. The sun streams
through limbs. Light and shadow puzzle
her face. *Heal means return.*

At Maeola's muddied feet rests a basin,
knee high and wide as a trunk—
X's scratched around the sides
like forgotten names or stick people
with their arms stretching toward sky.
Heal means recover.

She pulls the quilt from the washtub,
tangled herb and bulbs float
atop muddied water, blooming bushels,
miniature trees. Maeola looks again
and sees feet, ears and tongues.

The women echo each other,
these roots from Africa
from Africa, roots from...
These roots are like your fingers—
they've been disconnected,
what we do is grow them again.

Maeola Sweeps

Round and round the oval rug
circling her chest-table, the rings
of mauve and blue, the corners of her den,
the creases between walls and floor,
she sweeps down the door
and out to the walkway. Dust from dust,
she sweeps, her feet covered with soil.

Maeola leans on the broomstick,
straws brushing over toes,
her nightgown, a transparent
layer of cotton, sticking to her breasts,
her hair knotted in all directions. Maeola
skips her "mercy, Lords," the moment beyond
and nothing else fitting to be said,

but to see David one last time, to see
the son she sent chasing freedom, to wish
on this miracle he finds his way home.

Returning the Water

Pearl whispered at the river: We can cry now—
after years of holding streams inside us
till our bodies ballooned, until tears

disfigured arms and legs, till muscles
ached with too much weight, hearts distended
and blood thickened and thinned,

thinned and thickened, turning toward fire,
and with clotted chambers we felt
nothing at all—neither kisses nor strokes,

slaps nor embraces. Our voices wavering
we said, we can take anything—we are indestructible:
we have been beaten, battered, and bruised,

and not one drop has overflowed our eyes.
But now sisters, we can return
the water to where it should naturally be.

Doris

"Slavery is a living wound under a patchwork of scars."
—*Kwadwo Opoku-Agyemang*

She draped naked buildings with daydreams,
stepped over shattered glass that once
held liquor and flashing fantasy,
placed whole families in opened windows,
a portrait of mama, papa, cousins and grands,
renamed the made-up children,
gave them spirituals and kenté cloth
piecing in the puzzle with songs.

"Weren't we captives
not submitting slaves?
Remember we resisted.
We resisted."

She still saw the wounds from the Passage,
when Dahomey, Ebo and Asanti were stuffed
in the bowels of boats and the spines of grown
men and women were chained to curve like embryos,
light blocked from eyes, tongues struck silent,
so many days in darkness, we forgot our names.

"I keep a picture of the sun
tucked in the corner of my mind.
I said, I keep a picture of the sun,
the way it rises at home,
tucked in corner of my mind.
When they tell me, I must be born again,
I say, the Spirit never died."

These rocks be singing
out of their souls,
calling the names
of their strength;
Harriet,
Sojourner,
Sister Nanny
and you.
You be the rock.
All rocks
cry sometimes,
even rocks
take a break
and hum spirituals.

Ancestral Prayer

Re mem ber me

forehead and eyes

cheekbones
and
mouth

ears and chin

shoulders
and
bosom

elbows and hands

heart
and
navel

marrow and thighs

knees
and
toes

intact undiminished
complete composed
in your vision

vibrant and radiant
full bodied
and fully being

so I may be whole again
so I may behold
again myself

Baobab Fruits

I. FREEDOM BAPTIST

after Faith Ringgold's "The Church Picnic, 1987"

Seven families sit on home sown quilts
like cousins in Senegal whispering
among baobab branches. Woven baskets

take refuge under oak arms, as if the women
had just returned from market. But they
are dressed for Jesus in vivid patterns

of ruby, emerald and jade—
the ladies' hats stacked with fresh peonies,
the men in humble suits and Sunday smiles

lean toward gourds of yams, collard greens,
biscuits. A breeze pins a leaf to Sister Willie's
bosom and she starts a stumbling testimony,

I, I, I, that simmers like roots into spiritual.
I love the Lord he heard my cry.
Hums spill over into waves, hallelujahs echo,

tapping spines like God's blue breath.
Reverend Wright and Doris, the history
carrier, take to dancing: this is Freedom

Baptist's Picnic, Chicago, Illinois, 1909.
And an ocean away unripe fruits fall
from the baobab's grasp as if they heard names.

II. Missing Passage

I dis-remember the boat,

fierce swaying,

a shoreline slipping away.

I dis-remember a space

not meant for breathing,

my body spooned against strangers,

my voice falling faint,

punctured with holes

like a tattered flag.

I dis-remember shock

looping through my prayers

until they vanished.

I will out the boat

every day of the journey,

I ritualize forgetting.

From shore to shore,

my mind leaps, drawing blank

bridges, and I walk across them

saying, *over, over, over.*

III. BELOW DECK

They cannot prepare the body for burial, cannot
smooth the twisted face or draw closed her eyes.

Yet the woman locked to the dead one moans,
breaking her breath like a sacrifice.

And one by one the chained women chant,
mixing languages in their mouths,

words clicking behind their teeth. Song slips
over cracked lips as if oiling singed skin,

as if passing the frail body between them,
song soothes the soul's cry.

Locked in the belly of *Tomorrow's* ship, their voices
must do all, must be diligent hands, must

dress the deceased properly, mark her forehead
with white rings and braid her hair.

IV. DJALI

I recall burying them in trees—
our djalis, our history carriers.
In the pulp of baobabs,
we carved homes,
tucked bodies back
into birth positions
then sealed the trunks.

And for nine months, we kept
our ears to the ground
until we heard rustling
of soil and soul—
roots supping water,
sprouting buds' crackle
and the fruits' fleshy sigh.

V. CONJUR WOMAN

after Romare Bearden

She swapped cheeks
with the mountain lion,
raised patience like
evaporating water
and pawned faith
for a season of sleep
from dreaming bear.

Cotton-sack dress
cousin Tubman lent her
blended with patchwork
skin. Ruby and gold leaves
wrapping leathery
feet were crisp
and full of whispers.

I felt her staring,
tangled tree limbs
hiding her
like a woven shield,
centuries in her
collage face,

history etched in
folds of forehead,
right eye as piercing
as the hawk's,
left eye wild like
a spinning marble.

The Baobab

(Goreé Island, Senegal)

The kindred worry
Maison des Esclaves,
feel their way
through the chambers—
the stain of scarlet splotches,
the smell of iron and salt.

They halt and whisper
their names to stone-walls,
over and again—
Jackson, Johnson, Jones—
puzzle their fingers
along the vein-like cracks,

as if the walls
would start trembling,
break down and tell them
to whom they belong—
which people, which
river, which tree.

Sprouting Roots

What the tree witnessed was reason
enough to clench its roots and turn
the buried rock, to swell and coil
its roots under corners, to shift soil,
little by little tilting walls, making stone
cringe and crack, reason enough to unlevel
a slave house and furiously flower,
sprouting more roots to inch under
scorched sand and reach after
the Middle Passage—reason enough
to press through thunderous
tides, raise pieces of bone, cowrie shells
and anklets from the ocean floor, to sprawl up
mountains of waves, then disappear
at the shore and journey underground.

Coming Through

She comes in the mornings,
unbraiding my hair,
unweaving my thoughts.
While I shower she whispers,

"Feel what they did
to my body—
welts, marks, curses
carved in skin."

And Efa keeps appearing,
seeking healing
after centuries. She comes
through my hands,

fingering my face
like a blind person,
"Look at us, captured
in a passage of cruelty."

She moans,
and moans loudly,
as I pour palm oil
over my scalp,

rub ointment
on my skin,
and our blackness
glistens.

Rocking with arms
around my chest,
I comfort her and say,
 "Yes, but we are

coming through and look,
look at our beauty."

Oklahoma Quilt

I. PAINTING FLOWERS

The dead call me home for funerals.
I stroll the old roads,
now foreign, belonging to faces
known only by family resemblance,
the way orange reminds you of a dress,
the way rose talc powder
conjures up grandmother's hands.

Time is circling. At thirty-
three years old, I step
through the silver fence,
down the lawn to the little house,
inside there is a girl
with my face and birthmark.
I ask myself to come out,
out of Tulsa, out of this place
of bombs and riots.

But she smiles. There's yellow
watercolor on the paint brush
she holds like a thought.
And in that moment of years,
I remember picking a four-leaf clover
between train tracks, oaks
anchoring the backyard,
piano notes, cricket-filled nights.

She turns her head back
to great-grandmother's wall,
not at all surprised by my visit.
The little girl says, as kindly as possible,
I am painting flowers.

II. MOUNT ZION

after Tulsa Race Riot, 1921

Tobacco tucked in his left cheek,
he says: they burned Mount Zion.

Sister Wiley's spirit-driven voice
wasn't testifying, *Here I am, Lord.*

Deacon Mack wasn't thumbing through
his red-ink Bible looking for words.

No children in their Sunday best
were skipping past the pews.

Ms. Willie wasn't bending on arthritic
knees. Rose wasn't playing hopscotch in back.

Still, when they scorched Mount Zion,
they set the fire to the people.

III. WATER SONG

I wanted to come to you
in your cutting pain,
show you the medicine
hidden behind the cypress,
under heart-shaped tiger lily,
slide the branch of splinters
out of your brittle skin.

I wanted to lay hands over
your fractured chest,
sing the bones back together.
I was there when they swung
your body in the wind,
when they marked your spine
and punctured private parts.

I remember the burning,
the hot summer,
the torturous dying. Today,
when you sweat in the chill
of winter, I want to sprout
a fountain, like the hydrant
where children cool themselves—
to shower you in a water song.

IV. After

We brought those breathing home,
carried our hopes in our arms
like newborns and fragile elders,

back into the house, souped them
candied yams and survival tales,
until all were healthy and strong

again. And we never forgot our loss,
the open faces strewn on the path—
the shattered arms and legs and torsos.

And in the quilt of an Oklahoma night,
we dance our remembrance until we become
one river of blood, spirit, bones.

V. "NOTICE"

"Chief Sam is going back,
let another people mule this land,
never seen Africa before
but the soil shall know us.

"If you wish to be joined in wholeness,
meet at Henry's Dried Goods & Grocery,
Liberation Day of August, 1923,
bring money, canned foods and dreams."

VI. THE ILLNESS

We pretended not to notice
the thinning hair, sunken
cheeks, the blazer falling

off the shoulders.
Concealing the silence
with threads of chitchat,

we threw our eyes back
and laughed too wildly.
And for the first time

we said grace aloud,
ate the potluck—steamed
carrots and broccoli,

prayers continuing under
our breath, we swallowed
chicken breasts, petitions

salting our food, we pushed
yams in our cheeks, puckered
our mouths over lemonade,

but we meant mercy—mercy, God,
and we were afraid.
We were afraid.

VII. Joining the Oak

I kissed your cheek, Papa,
your body seven days dead.

Hoping the touch would sugar-coat
the life passed, straighten out misunderstood years

the way a young man adjusts his tie
or a mother worries a room to perfection.

On your pasty eyelids, I saw flecks
of an unwanted child, the father who lost a son,

the body living with ailing spirit.
The kiss, old habit, on seeing

your slight smile, but this time,
my lips turned numb, my tongue

weighed like earth in my mouth.
I could feel the seasons change,

and everyone vanishing inside of trees: you
joining the broad oak at the lake's edge,

me, on the outside, circling
maples, elms and willows.

VIII. PENNY JAR

With the inheritance, I bought a haunted gown,
wedded with your memories and dreams.

You schooled a wide-eyed college
girl about the Tulsa riot of '21—

thirty-five blocks of homes smoldered into ashes,
Booker T. High became a hospital,

firebomb mushrooms bruised the sky.
The sudden blinks of your eyelids told

what your mouth wouldn't say
as you chewed words and spat tobacco.

And the green chair is still there, Papa,
and the red coffee spit can with half the Folger's

label peeled off, and black houseshoes
with your footprints, and your stories:

whispering through Nefertari's tiara
I donned on my wedding day

as the gown's tulle train ghosted
me down the church aisle.

Carrying Home

I am carrying home in my breast pocket:
land where I learned to crawl,
dust that held my footprints,
long fields I trod through.

Home, where Mother baked bread,
where Papa spoke with skies,
where family voices gathered.
In my palm, this heap of earth
I have hauled over hills and valleys.

Releasing dirt between my fingers,
I ask the prairies to sustain me.
May my soil and this soil nurture each other,
may seeds root and develop beyond measure,
may the heartland and I blossom.

But she has strength and steadfast hardihood.
Deep-rooted is she, even as the oaks,
Hardy as perennials about her door.
The circle of the seasons brings no fear.

Sterling A. Brown, "Virginia Portrait"

Streams of Sapphire

After they lower him into the broken ground,
after the proverbs and wailing,
after the Sistas in Jesus fry chicken wings,

the sun pokes a ray under her kitchen curtain,
and caresses her chin with warmth,
but she swats the sign like bees

and continues pressing his shirts,
shining his Sunday shoes, fluffing
the feathered pillow he made himself, anyhow.

Every now and then, their favorite tune comes
floating out the radio box and her tongue
slips his name, like he's just shaving,
or in back rubbing ointment on his knees.

One day, while she's sipping coffee,
a blueness appears, wanders freely
through the den. Tears soak her hanky.
"I knew you would come, I knew you would come."

She pampers him more this time,
sits up nights roaring out memories,
and sometimes she dances a *slow drag,*

then snickering like a girl,
she cups her hand over a toothless smile,
"I couldn't forget you, sho' couldn't forget."

When grandbaby visits she minds,
"Say hello to your grandfather." No harm,
she toys, *"he wasn't ready to leave no how,*
ugly cancer ate his body, stole his sweet breath."

"Now, he's strong, sturdy, blue like dawn,
and we still be together," she grins.
"Same as before, who says we can't?"

Her skin fades to indigo,
and when you knock on the side door,
you aren't sure who's answering—he or she?

But clouds smother the house for certain.
Grandbaby grows to know her Papa well,
instead of a gravestone with a name

his Mama called him, printed across,
she knows him as he is, streams of sapphire.

Distant Rain

Mama's eyes are turning to clouds.
She forgets the way to the grocery store.
Broccoli rots in the bread box.

Some days she does not know me—
these shoulders she's sponged in the river,
the baby hands she taught to hold water.

Unpinning her cinnamon-roll plaits,
she's chasing light-bugs for diamonds
and playing pitty-pat with playmates.

She paces the Trail of Tears with Daddy
strapped to her back and yellow irises
neatly folded into the Book of Job.

Lying in bed, grey cush crowning her shoulders,
she whispers of her mother and lilacs,
the room quilted with fading photographs.

At dawn her eyes rest on the clouds,
emerging spirits pushing up the sun,
and she waves, sadness outlining her smile.

And we stroll around the tomato garden,
chanting names of old and new friends coming,
like a distant sheet of rain, to take her home.

First Day

My sister and I crossed the train tracks
after school and started back on the dirt road,

gazing at the field of sunflowers, their stems
tall as giraffes reaching toward the possible.

Butterflies hopscotched on waving grass
while we skipped toward Miss Luella's biscuits.

And with every step, we disremembered
the National Guard pointing and ordering

the principal to open the school doors,
the girl with sausage curls spitting and crying,

the teacher re-naming us pickaninnies.
We rose when the bell trembled,

straightened our faces and spines, wrapped
our arms around each other's spirits

and forgave God for being absent-
minded and not meeting us that day.

Migrations

The diesel truck grunts to pick up the house, to
ease the residence onto its broad back, to haul *1619*

whole down the highway. The home—wobbles
without foundation, trembles by sudden movement,

by turbulence and blurring trees, is disturbed
by groundlessness. It wavers and hiccups,

reduced to numbers on a flapping door,
no Little Africa or Creek Center claiming its walls.

After this crossing from South to North, will
wooden floors hold when the truck settles them?

Will walls endure after being upswept or will
the house crack to pieces? What of the father

driving the Buick, the mother unwrapping
sandwiches, the children in the backseat singing?

Integration

after Countee Cullen

One childhood day
in my new neighborhood—
while freely circling
bouncing butterflies
and giggling at
the daffodil's story—

a child in white
ruffles interrupted me
and wiped a forefinger
down my outstretched arm,
asking, "How do you know
when you're dirty?"

The Trip Over

With knees pressed to chest,
she flashes to the smell
of ships, carcasses,

urine flowing stronger
than old outhouses
in the South.

To damp bodies moaning,
packed below deck, in one
position spooned west,

bones lock after time, even
ten-year-old knees pop,
when allowed to stand.

And it rushes back to her
when lying on the waterbed
before pulling up the covers.

Rona

Rona wasn't supposed to be the one.
Anchor swung over the eldest,
hooked the middle child.

She plopped up, still plump
with baby fat, popped
her thumb out of mouth,

tied a knot in the holy apron,
wore ridges in the rug
toting Blue Baby.

She broke the green beans' backs,
peeled the flimsy spines,
scraped the soiled tub.

And she looks like a grown up
with pink barrettes
in her plaits, but she is nine.

She forgets London Bridges,
she forgets hopscotch,
she forgets to laugh

the way Aunt smothers joy
as Jehovah's witness.
Rona means business.

And she didn't cry
after Mama died,
or tote her favorite toys.

To keep her heart warm,
she dangles Salems
from the curve of tiny lips

where Mama's kisses went,
and coughs through puffs
about work and no time,

with propped-opened
eyes, afraid to blink
because a river swells

under her eyelids,
and Blue Baby could
drown in her lap.

And Rona could be washed
back into childhood,
and who would be Mama

and who would be Papa,
and who would be Mama,
and who would be Papa,

if Rona were only a young girl?

"My Mama's Light"

after a sculpture by Marva Pitchford Jolly

She gathered some clay and pressed out a face—
I'm telling you what my heart felt—
took her pinkie nail and pried nose holes

in all that grayness, look like earth breathing,
and no body attached, just two faces
propped on the balls of their skulls.

And she rounded more mud in her palms,
rolled it gently between caked hands,
and I heard chanting over the river

where Africans and Cherokees
gather to swap stories and remedies.
It hasn't happened for sixty-five years—

but I'm telling you I heard the story of healing
when she rubbed her palms. And when she stood
the third piece of ground on end,

I smelled Mother's breath rising from the head's lips,
all minty the way it smells when she's singing
with her eyes closed and right foot patting.

And from behind the maple they cut down
five years ago, Uncle Jim shouted,
and out came the spirits.

Hydrangeas

for Gwendolyn Brooks

Great-Mama took such care tending
the teal hydrangeas—their massive heads,
full of petals like impulsive thoughts,
could fly apart in any spring breeze
and they would be left scattered, half
of themselves, and still appear full-headed.
Great-Mama nursed them with formulas,
whispered names and lullabies
under her breath, patted and cooed
the soil at the roots until her palms
were caked black. Oh, how they blossomed
and sprouted, framing the front yard
as if to say, she is ours, ours, to touch her
you must cross from flesh to flower.

Jesus And B. B. King

There was always music
in my house.

I said: There was always music
in my house.

The floors stood up and
called out for song.

I said: The floors stood up and
called out for song.

When the record player broke,
the icebox hummed the song.

When the record player broke,
I said: the icebox hummed along.

We called on King, in my house.
B. B. by first name.

I'm sure he's one of
God's plans.

The blues and Jesus
went hand in hand.

I said: The blues and Jesus
went hand in hand.

Ask Jesus or King,
whichever one you can.

Oh, yeah, they'll tell you,
Come on over to my house.

Delivery

Before leaving home to deliver mail,
he stands in front of his mirror,
half-dressed, half-father, half-worker,
dots of grey framing his hairline,
his eyebrows growing together.
He studies his eyes—
if they smile when he doesn't,
if they fly away when he squints.
He studies the edges of his mouth,
the stubble on his chin demanding care.
And though nothing will need to be spoken
to complete the ten-hour workshift,
he tries his voice—
it is melodic, robust, full,
the humming of workers everywhere.

Shadow Man Chants

Shadow Man chants of soldiers,
of vipers crawling in the fields
and fire beetles tickling his nose.

He wraps words with home-drawn honey,
puts on brother's smile and tells
of more than separated arms and legs,

of minds disconnected from souls.
Shadow Man chants and stars fall
from his eyes. And we mean not

to see, not to listen, but he sure looks
like Bill and talks with a preacher's drawl
like Paul, got a slanted shoulder like Jim.

Shadow's songs strike like death
in a wedding dress, something beautiful
about his voice—we gasp for breath

and ask more—so that's how them boys died.
Tell us more, Shadow Man,
your chants forming icicles in our chests.

Young Girl Dancing

Men sat crooked on fire-red barstools,
clutching shots with forefinger and thumb
like deacons grip communion on Sunday,

cigarettes hanging from the hook of lips—
sizzling into ashy grey snakes,
tainting breath and ghosting stubby faces.

And she was standing on the toes of tennis
shoes, winding hips and weaving thighs,
knees pushing forward, pelvis pulsing,

budding breast bouncing up and down
with the arch and straightening of spine.
Just like Jill when we play in gym class.

Blue jeans was blue, was lingerie, black teddy.
She bopped to the spot under the strobe light
and her body became electrified,

her face metallic and she was girlfriend, secretary,
young wife, the woman in the pink mini and tall
heels crossing Seventh Street.

And tonight, she was enough woman at twelve
for the slew nursing Jack Daniels
escaping the janitor mops, the mailroom bin,

the service desk, the hotel's front door.
She blew a huge bubble out of grape gum,
poked out her tongue, wiped the sweat-beads

from smooth forehead and separated
herself to the rising beat and breaking lights,
the smoky shadows whooping and grinning,

grinning and whooping while inching closer—
an audience to her, an offering to them.
And the air ran home to tell Mama.

Blues Song

after Ayi Kwei Armah

I heard we once all prayed together,
now division roams.
I heard we once all prayed together,
now division roams.
Somebody said two thousand seasons,
before we free home.

Lordy, Lordy, Lord,
don't take that long.
Lordy, Lordy, Lord,
I said, don't take that long.
That's too many centuries
singing the same song.

Heal this illness now, Lord,
just set it loose.
I pray, heal this illness now, Lord,
lay your hands and set it loose.
You unchained my body, Lord,
unlock my mind, too.

Coming Home

Look, Taylor's coming home
after years of building invisible fences,
of moseying straight by Mother's place
and Aunt Pearlie's pink peony yard,
after ivied universities, foreign cars
and talking different tongues, none religious.

Taylor's coming home, hand pressed to chest,
saying Muskogee can't be matched,
saying the other places seemed odd,
he learned as much from Papa's
domino club and Rudie's psychic dog,
saying he always loved me (now get that).

My man's home and all I can do is cry—
some from spite, some from confusion,
some 'cause it pained me so when he left—
but I sing through the stirring dust,
"Mr. Taylor, come on in this house!" I fluff
pillows like welcoming arms, and smooth
the wave from my violet dress.

Hands

When they told us we could have each other,
I didn't know what to do, how to hold you.
I hadn't embraced anyone in years.

I had lost my hands to scrubbing,
stirring, and scraping fabric against iron.
I hadn't used them for touching since Philip
pushed out of me thirty-five years ago.

These hands aren't hands, they're just tools
used for cleaning what's never gonna come clean,
with dirt being thrown in the wind.

But I'm gonna stretch them out anyway
to see how you feel. You've been tucked
in my heart all of this time and I've loved
you longer than I've had wooden hands.

Wet Oak

He be a home mender and floor fixer,
his laugh come up fluttering from his root
and he tremble so, sprinklings of joy
like fall leaves, float over the kitchen.
He no high yellow nor big muscle man,
he the color of wet oak after dry season,
then rain come splattering with deep kisses
like tree and ground was a virgin again
and even hidden spots be holding water.
His hands, broad and playful, fill with dreams
that unfold and talk through his silence.
He a man without trying too hard,
with eyes that go soft around sadness
and dance when he watching the galaxy.
He ain't afraid to do some crying
and talk about some old wrongs and hurts.
He let his voice go high as mine
and fall to baritone when he's happy.
When he rises, he's sturdy as oaks
that have conquered all seasons.

About the Author

Angela Shannon's poetry has been published in *TriQuarterly, Ploughshares* and other magazines, and her choreopoem, "Root Woman," premiered at the Fleetwood-Jourdain Theater in Evanston, Illinois, in 2001. She has won a poetry fellowship from the Illinois Arts Council and a Mentor Award from The Loft in Minneapolis, where she has also taught. She received an MFA in poetry from Warren Wilson College.